DISCARD

10-minute

SEASONAL

CRAFTS

for

AUTUMN

ANNALEES LIM

WINDMILL BOOKS

New York

Published in 2015 by Windmill Books, An Imprint of Rosen Publishing
29 East 21st Street, New York, NY 10010

Senior Editor for Wayland: Julia Adams
Craft stylist: Annalees Lim
Designer: Emma Randall
Photographer: Simon Pask, N1 Studios

Photo Credits: All step-by-step craft photography: Simon Pask, N1 Studios; images used throughout for creative graphics: Shutterstock.

Library of Congress Cataloging-in-Publication Data

Lim, Annalees, author.
 10-minute seasonal crafts for autumn / by Annalees Lim.
     pages cm. — (10-minute seasonal crafts)
 Includes index.
 ISBN 978-1-4777-9214-8 (library binding) — ISBN 978-1-4777-9215-5 (pbk.) —
ISBN 978-1-4777-9216-2 (6-pack)
 1. Handicraft—Juvenile literature. 2. Autumn—Juvenile literature. I. Title.
 TT160.L48492 2015
 745.5—dc23
                            2013048366

Manufactured in the United States of America

CPSIA Compliance Information: Batch # WS14WM: For Further Information contact Windmill Books, New York, New York at 1-866-478-0556

Contents

AUTUMN

Autumn is one of the seasons of the year. The months of autumn are September, October and November.

During the autumn months the days get shorter and colder. The green scenes of summer slowly turn to red, orange and brown. Leaves fall from trees, getting blown around in the gusty winds. Some small creatures prepare to hibernate for the long cold winter by collecting lots of food and material with which to make dens.

Autumn is a really exciting time of year and there is much to explore outside. Whether it's jumping through piles of dried leaves or sitting by bonfires, you won't want to stay inside for long!

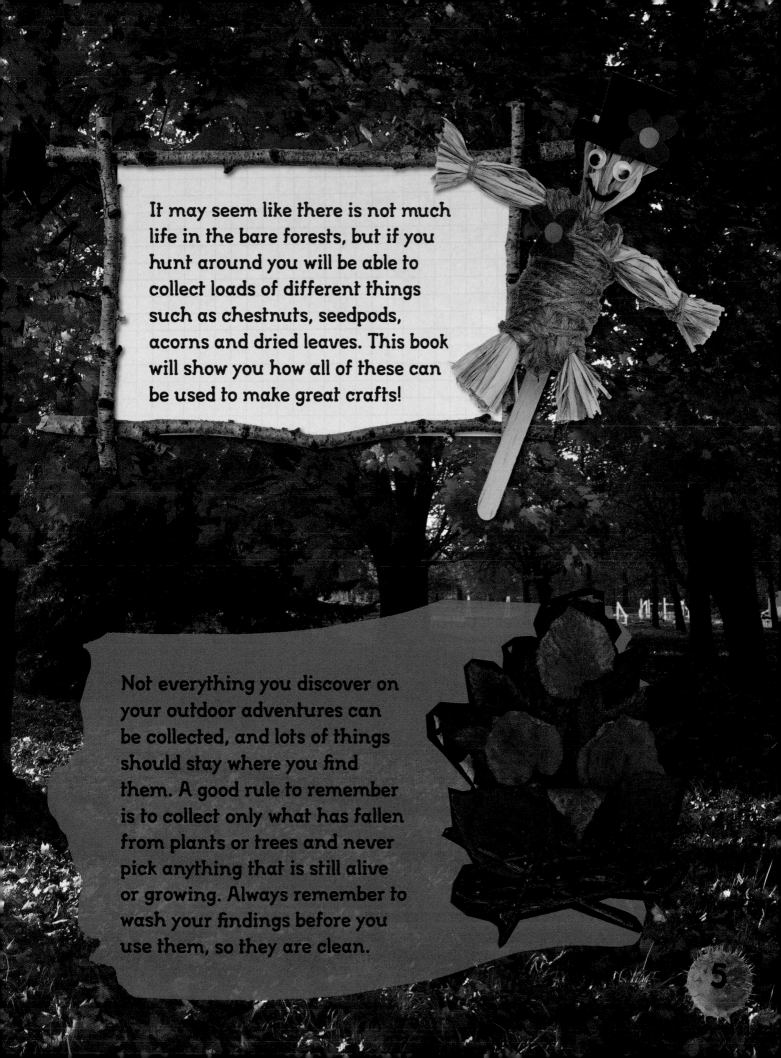

It may seem like there is not much life in the bare forests, but if you hunt around you will be able to collect loads of different things such as chestnuts, seedpods, acorns and dried leaves. This book will show you how all of these can be used to make great crafts!

Not everything you discover on your outdoor adventures can be collected, and lots of things should stay where you find them. A good rule to remember is to collect only what has fallen from plants or trees and never pick anything that is still alive or growing. Always remember to wash your findings before you use them, so they are clean.

5

Pinecone Squirrel

Squirrels scurry around busily in autumn, collecting fallen acorns, so they have a good supply of food for the winter. Make your own scavenging squirrel out of a pinecone and an acorn that you have found on a walk in the woods.

You will need:

- Pinecone
- 7 brown pipe cleaners
- Acorn
- Glue
- Googly eyes

1 Wrap a pipe cleaner around a pinecone to create some arms. Bend them into shape.

2 Do the same with another pipe cleaner to make the legs and feet.

3

Make some ears and a nose by wrapping the pipe cleaner around the top of the cone and bending it into shape.

4

Make a fluffy tail using four folded pipe cleaners and stick them onto the bottom of the cone.

5

Stick some googly eyes onto the face and an acorn between the squirrel's hands.

Freshly fallen pinecones are often still closed. If you collect these, just keep them somewhere warm such as a sunny windowsill until they have opened up and are ready to use.

Apple Hedgehog Prints

Autumn is harvest time, and lots of apples are picked at this time of year. Apples are very tasty, but some that you find on the ground may not be good to eat. Instead, use them to make this fun craft!

You will need:

- Blue and green paper
- Scissors
- Glue
- Apple
- Small pinecone
- Dark and light brown paint
- Paintbrush
- Brown card stock or paper
- Pen
- Googly eyes

1 Cut a border of green grass and stick it onto a blue sheet of paper.

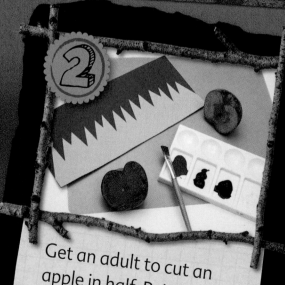

2 Get an adult to cut an apple in half. Paint the center of the cut surface light brown, and the edges dark brown.

3 Press the apple half onto the paper three times to make three prints. You may have to reapply the paint.

4 Dip a small pinecone in some dark brown paint to add some bristles around the apple prints.

5 Cut out three faces using some brown card stock or paper. Stick them onto the hedgehog bodies and add some googly eyes.

Dried Leaf Bonfire

People often make bonfires in the autumn to burn the leaves they have collected in their garden. Why not gather some dried leaves and make your very own crafty bonfire?

You will need:
- Red, yellow and brown leaves
- Black card stock
- Glue
- Sticks
- White paint
- Pencil

Stick some red leaves onto a black piece of card stock.

Bonfires are made from piles of dead leaves and also make an inviting home for animals such as hedgehogs. It is very important to check the pile for these animals before you light a fire.

Find some smaller yellow leaves and stick them on top of the red ones.

3 Glue some brown leaves at the bottom of the red and yellow leaves.

4 Glue some sticks to the bottom of the leaf flames. These are the logs for your fire.

5 Dip a pencil into some white paint and print some sparkly stars in the dark sky.

11

Field Mouse

Corn is grown in fields and can grow very tall. It is a great place for field mice to nest. They are shy animals, so you are lucky if you manage to spot one. Why not make your own field mouse using straw or corn you have gathered?

You will need:
- orange, yellow and blue paper
- Glue
- Scissors
- Straw or corn
- Light and dark brown felt
- Tape
- Googly eyes

1 Cut out some jagged shapes from orange and yellow paper and stick them onto some blue paper.

2 Stick a line of corn or straw along the bottom of the paper using tape.

3 Use the dark brown felt to make the body and tail of the field mouse.

4 Cut a triangle for the ear and a nose from the light brown felt and stick all of the parts of the field mouse on top of the corn.

5 Glue a googly eye to the mouse.

Try making a whole field of corn, and instead of making an animal that lives in it, try making some flying crows out of black felt. Stick them onto the sky above your corn field.

Spider Web

Autumn mornings are often very chilly, and if you look early enough in the morning you can easily spot spider webs sparkling with dew or frost. If you haven't woken up early enough to see the webs for yourself, collect some sticks and make your own spider web!

You will need:

- 4 sticks
- String
- 4 pipe cleaners
- A pom pom
- Googly eyes
- Scissors
- Glue

1

Choose four sticks that are similar in size.

2

Tie two sticks together to make a cross. Do the same with the other two sticks.

3 Tie the two crossed sticks together to make a star shape.

4 Use your string to make the web. Start by tying the string to one stick and winding it around each stick in turn until it looks like a web.

5 Take the four pipe cleaners and twist them together in the middle. Bend each into an 'm' shape and add the pom pom and some googly eyes.

If you have some extra pipe cleaners you can make some flies that have been caught up in the spider web. You could make their wings out of some white tissue paper.

Mini Owls

On a quiet evening you sometimes hear an owl hooting. If you are really lucky you may even see one soaring through the sky. If you can find lots of acorns outside, you can make your own gathering of owls.

You will need:

- Acorns
- Modeling clay
- Scissors
- Googly eyes
- Glue
- Colored paper or card stock
- Colored pencil

1 Roll a small piece of yellow modeling clay into a ball and press your acorn into it.

2 Using some scissors, cut into the modeling clay to make some claws.

3

Stick some googly eyes onto the acorn.

4

Make a beak using more modeling clay and press it onto the acorn.

5

Cut out some paper wings and draw on some feathers. Stick these to the owl's sides.

17

Scarecrow

Scarecrows are used to scare crows away from fields of crops. You can make your own mini scarecrow from corn that you have collected from a walk in the countryside or straw that you use for your pet's bedding.

You will need:
- straw
- string
- scissors
- popsicle stick
- colored paper or card stock
- googly eyes
- glue

1 Take a handful of straw, fold it in half and secure it in place by tying some string around the top. This part will form the head.

If you can't find any straw to use for this craft, you could buy some raffia. This can be bought from most florists.

2 Separate the rest of the straw into four parts. Tie the two outside bundles, using string to make the arms and hands. Do the same with the other two bundles to make the legs and feet.

3

Place a popsicle stick at the back and wrap string around it to make it stay in place.

4

Trim the hands and feet using scissors.

5

Use colored card stock to make a paper hat and some paper flowers. Stick them onto your scarecrow, along with some googly eyes.

Book Worm

Autumn days are shorter and it gets dark earlier in the evening. If it's cold outside, sometimes there is nothing better than curling up with a good book. Use some leaves to make a fun bookmark that you can use through the dark autumn evenings.

1 Choose five large round leaves and stick them onto some tape.

2 Stick the tape with the leaves onto a piece of card stock. Draw a worm shape and a pair of glasses using a permanent marker.

3 Cut around the shape to make the body of the book worm.

4 Decorate the book worm with sticky dots.

5 Add some googly eyes and a smile.

You can use leaves to make lots of different patterns and shapes for your bookmark. Try making a small mouse or maybe a bear, ready to hibernate.

Chestnut Creatures

Chestnuts grow on trees. You can find them once they have fallen to the ground. They can be found in woods, parks and even on streets. If you find they are not soft enough to use for this craft, just soak them in water for an hour or so.

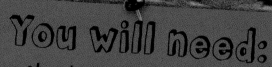

You will need:
- chestnuts
- Toothpicks
- Modeling clay
- Googly eyes

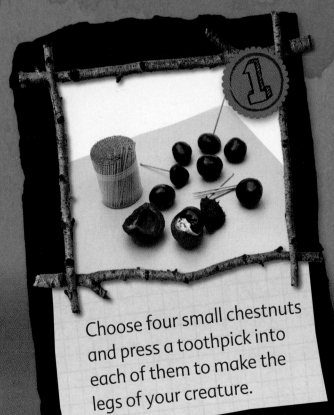

1

Choose four small chestnuts and press a toothpick into each of them to make the legs of your creature.

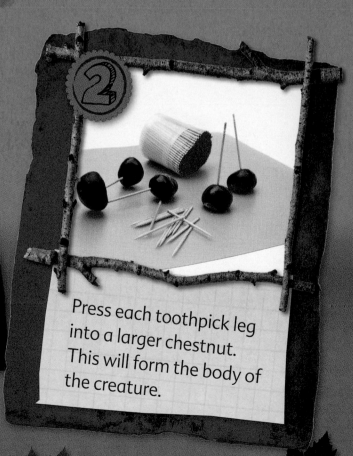

2

Press each toothpick leg into a larger chestnut. This will form the body of the creature.

3 Make a head and tail in the same way you made the legs.

4 Press some googly eyes onto the head using a bit of modeling clay.

5 Press small balls of modeling clay onto the body to make colorful dots.

23

Glossary

den (DEN) A wild animal's home.

dew (DOO) Tiny drops of water that form on things during the night.

florist (FLOR-ist) A shopkeeper who sells flowers.

frost (FROST) Powdery ice that forms on things in freezing weather.

gather (GATH-ur) To collect.

harvest (HAR-vist) The time when farmers gather the corn, fruit and vegetables they have grown.

hibernate (HY-bur-nayt) When an animal goes to sleep for the winter

scavenge (SKA-venj) To search for useful things, such as food.

soak (SOHK) To place something in liquid, such as water.

Index

Further Reading

Appleby, Alex. *What Happens in Fall? Four Super Seasons*. New York: Gareth Stevens, 2014.

Barnham, Kay. *Fall. Season*. New York: PowerKids Press, 2011.

Websites

For web resources related to the subject of this book, go to: www.windmillbooks.com/weblinks and select this book's title.

24